Mindful

Meditate & Color Your Way to Life-Giving Relationships

Deb Potts

Illustrated by Macy Simmons

Dear friends, let us love one another,

for love comes from God.

1 JOHN 4:7

DO NOT *READ* THIS DEVOTIONAL!

This devotional was not written to be read, it was written to be experienced.

In Mindful, you will embark on a rich contextual journey, pursuing abundance in your relationships. Renew and enhance life-filled connection to God, yourself, and other people by engaging all your senses.

Not only will you learn by reading and applying the meditations, but as movement anchors thought, you will give form and beauty to your understanding when you color the charming "doodles" by Macy Simmons (www.etsy.com/shop/writtenontheheart423).

I'm a messy reader - I love to scribble in the margins and highlight the books I read. I honestly cannot read without a pen in my hand. If you are like me, I've given you extra wide margins. Scribble away to your heart's content. It's ok, really! I've included a framed box for each entry where you can jot down what God is saying to you on that page. When you pray, don't forget to pause and listen – God longs to connect with you in sacred intimacy. Just ask: God, what do you want me to know about this? Then make sure to write down what you sense Him saying. He's just waiting for you to ask.

I love to experience God with all my senses. That way, I am better able to be present, be peaceful, and be awake! I can remember what I read for more than 15 minutes. Here are some suggestions to enhance your meditations.

Engage your sense of smell. Incense was burned at times of prayer in the Bible. God speaks of our prayers as having a beautiful aroma. Use essential oils, either in a diffuser or apply them to your skin. You may have your favorites, or you could try a new one. Biblical essential oils include frankincense, myrrh, and cassia. Peppermint is good if you fear nodding off, and lavender is great for relieving anxiety.

Engage your sense of hearing. I use a sound app on my phone to keep me focused. My mind tends to wander, and the sounds help me. I love water sounds, because God's voice is compared to the sound of many waters in the Bible. Rainfall, waves, rivers, and waterfalls all give me a sense of peace. I also love sounds of the outdoors. Birdsong, crickets, and frogs are soothing and peaceful. So are campfire sounds, a heartbeat or windchimes. Experiment with different sounds.

Engage your sense of taste. The Bible says to taste and see that the Lord is good in Psalm 34:8. Even if someone eloquently describes how an apple tastes, we will never experience it until we bite into one. Don't just imagine what God is like, really experience Him. I most often struggle with distraction, so I like to have caffeine when I'm meditating. I love both coffee and tea, and recommend what works for you. Caffeine-free teas that can help with distraction and focus include mint, lemon, and ginger. If you feel anxious, try chamomile or passion flower.

I haven't dated the devotions either, for Heaven's sake! Who wants to feel like they failed at reading a devo if they skipped a day? I hope you totally consume this book – that when you finish it in a month or a year it's falling apart at the seams. Use it, scribble in it – get every last drop of it until you're filled up and starving for more of God.

Think of how you developed a craving for chocolate. The more you eat of it the more you want it. That's how it works with God too. The more you have of Him, the more you want of Him. Develop a craving for God!

Visit debpotts.com/mindful for more information.

This devotional is a companion to my book, Making Peace with Prickly People: Transforming Relationships by Loving God, Self, and Others. If you enjoy this book, you will want to grab some girlfriends and go through the free study guide.

Visit pricklypeople.com for freebies including Personality Key (a personality assessment), a Prickly People Prayer Calendar, and a 6-week study guide.

CONTENTS

1

MARK 12:28B - 30

Of all the commandments, which is the most important?

A most important question about the most important commandment. Jesus answered the question in Mark 12 by saying, "Love God with all your heart, all your soul, all your mind, and all your strength."

God, it turns out, invented love. How surprising that the inventor of love would want rebellious people to love Him back. Or maybe that's not so surprising. He watches us from heaven, His heart on His sleeve. The most powerful force in the universe is a sucker for the very love He invented.

Be mindful about making peace with God. He sent His loving son, Jesus, to make peace with us. What does that look like in your life?

The 'Love God' section of this devotional will help you unpack what this means. But before we get started, reflect for a moment: what does it look like to love God in these ways?

Notice the passage doesn't say love God with ½ your heart, ¼ of your soul, most of your mind, and a smidgeon of your strength. It's 'all.' This speaks of commitment and balance. Like: "I'm in this all the way."

Notice also that the passage doesn't say love God with all "the" heart, soul, mind, and strength. Rather, it's "your" heart, soul, mind, and strength. Each of us is different, uniquely created. My heart may look different than your heart. Isn't it reassuring God allows us to love Him as uniquely as He created us?

Think of the ways you show love to God. What does that look like? Do you truly love Him? Would you like to?

What God is saying to me....

2

MARK 12:31

The second is this: "Love your neighbor as yourself." There is no commandment greater than these.

Honestly, who in the world really loves their neighbor this much? I've spent a lifetime learning how to do that and I've failed over and over again.

However, since this is the second most important rule in God's economy it's probably pretty important.

Loving my neighbor is really about loving myself. My true identity can be masked by guilt, shame, and feeling "less-than." Sometimes we become our own worst enemies and we struggle to find anything lovable about ourselves. I might feel it isn't safe to be me, so I work hard to be someone else. But the mask never fits quite right.

Join me on a journey as we ponder love through the lens of personality, the personality of Jesus and the personality of people.

Before we get started, what thoughts come to mind when you think of 'personality?' How would you describe the personality of Jesus? How would you describe your personality? Have you ever taken a personality assessment? To help you understand your own personality, try the free assessment at pricklypeople.com.

What God is saying to me....

PART ONE:
LOVE GOD

3

ISAIAH 9:6

For to us a child is born, to us a son is given, and the government will be on his shoulders. And he will be called Wonderful Counselor, Mighty God, Everlasting Father, Prince of Peace.

Before choosing their baby's name, most parents consult a baby name website. Names always have meanings; they describe a person's destiny and life purpose. Biblical names are the same. It's not surprising that Jesus, the perfect Man, would need not just one name, but four names. Each of these four names represents a role He will play in leading mankind.

"...Wonderful Counselor, Mighty God, Everlasting Father, Prince of Peace..." Four names, four roles, four sides of the same person. We could think of these names as representing the four personality types. Since the ancient Greek physician, Hippocrates, most researchers support a four-fold personality model. This model can be applied to Jesus, the Perfect Man.

Have you experienced the wisdom of the Wonderful Counselor? Think back to when you received a new perspective as you contemplated God's word. Or maybe you have a question for the Wonderful Counselor today. If He were sitting next to you right now, what would you ask Him?

Have you ever encountered the Mighty God as He answered impossible prayers? In what area of your life do you need a mountain-shaking Mighty God today?

Do you long to crawl up into the lap of your Everlasting Father and feel His comfort? Is it forgiveness or compassion or something else you seek from Him?

Or do you just need to find peace in your chaos today? Your Prince of Peace is ready to go to battle for you, defeating the powers that bring pandemonium. Just ask Him; He's the listener, after all.

What God is saying to me...

4

MATTHEW 9:11

When the Pharisees saw this, they asked his disciples, "Why does your teacher eat with tax collectors and sinners?"

Everlasting Father; the compassionate, optimistic Heart of God. This title is the only one representing a family relationship. Jesus is the Perfect Father, not like our earthly, imperfect fathers. Our earthly fathers are not eternal, they rarely live as long as their children. And our earthly fathers have imperfect, selfish love. They may try to be good fathers, and some really are, but there's only one Good Father.

Jesus sees our potential. He created us in His image and loves to see His traits exhibited in us. It thrills Him when we delight in our true identity.

People (especially prickly people) will often love us conditionally. In other words, they expect something back. Like obedience, loyalty, or love.

Loving others unconditionally is hard. Loving unconditionally means to love expecting nothing in return. Not even love.

That's how the Everlasting Father loves us. There are no conditions under which He will stop loving us. No matter how many times we mess up, no matter what our reputation has become, no matter how many people have rejected us, our Everlasting Father will always be ready to welcome us with open arms.

"Are you hurting and broken within, overwhelmed by the weight of the sin, Jesus is calling. Have you come to the end of yourself, do you thirst for a drink from the well, Jesus is calling. O come to the altar, the Father's arms are open wide." From "O Come to the Altar", by Elevation Worship.

What do you have to confess today? Just ask Him to forgive you, He's been waiting for that all along. His arms are wide open, ready to wrap you in a huge bear hug.

5

MATTHEW 7:7

Ask and it will be given to you; seek and you will find; knock and the door will be opened to you.

Jesus is the Prince of Peace, the Soul of God. He answers prayers. He's a humble servant who came to bring peace to us.

The word "peace" in Hebrew is "shalom." Most would say shalom means peace. But, the word has over 70 meanings, and when taken in total it means completeness or wholeness.

Our Prince of Shalom is a whole, complete human man and an eternal God at the same time. He serves the people He created and sacrifices Himself for our good. Most importantly, He listens to our prayers and mediates between us and God.

God invites us into a sacred intimacy with Him through prayer. He knows all things, but He invites us to tell Him about our lives anyway.

In James 1, God gives wisdom "to all men generously and without reproach". There are no conditions under which God will not give wisdom if we ask. But then James goes on to say that if we doubt God, we will never receive the wisdom.

It's like we are on a cell phone call, and just as our friend is giving us her address, we lose the reception. She speaks the address into the phone, but we never hear it.

How many times have you prayed but it didn't seem that you received an answer? If you're like me, it's way too many times to count. It wasn't until I stopped talking and started to listen to God that I began to hear answers to my questions.

Remember that God gave us two ears and only one mouth. When you are praying to God, try listening twice as long as you speak. Don't doubt that you will hear from God, or that He can answer. What is your most burning question? Ask Jesus and then quietly and expectantly wait for the answer.

What God is saying to me...

6

MATTHEW 12:36

But I tell you that everyone will have to give account on the day of judgment for every empty word they have spoken.

Jesus is the Wonderful Counselor, the Mind of God. When you think of the incredible balance, intricacies, and beauty of nature as well as the complexity of our bodies, you get just an inkling of the extent of the Mind of God.

The Wonderful Counselor is a perfectionist, and a judge. Jesus perfectly carried out His agenda on earth, fulfilling every single prophecy written about Him. And He carefully takes note of every word, thought, and action of every person.

When you think of the "bad guys", those who have abused, murdered, and cheated others, aren't you glad that someday, someone is going to call them out? You know what types of people I mean, those prickly people! Sometimes it seems like they just get away with murder, however, in the end they will be held accountable.

But it's not quite so comfortable that the Wonderful Counselor is also keeping track of every empty word I have spoken.

As a follower of Jesus, I am forgiven, and will never lose my standing with God. My place in heaven is assured. And instead of cringing with fear at the thought that I will be called on the carpet for my words, thoughts, and deeds, I appreciate it as a wake-up call. In my prayers I often ask God to hold me accountable and alert me when I sin.

Confession is a cleansing act, removing the baggage that separates me from God. In Psalm 32 David shares that when he kept his sin a secret, it was like his bones were wasting away, his strength was sapped. Is there a secret sin you've been hiding? God already knows all about it. Can you muster up your courage and confess to Him? All you have to do is ask, and it will be forgiven. He already knows all about it, just tell him the truth.

What God is saying to me...

7
ISAIAH 61:1

The Spirit of the Sovereign Lord is on me, because the Lord has anointed me to proclaim good news to the poor. He has sent me to bind up the broken-hearted, to proclaim freedom for the captives and release from darkness for the prisoners.

Jesus is the Mighty God, the Strength of God. He is a powerful, valiant warrior who commands even the wind and waves. There is nothing He can't do. Jesus is also called the Lion of Judah, the King of Kings, and the Messiah. He is the best leader that ever was.

This passage of Scripture names three types of people who are present in our broken world. Jesus was sent to address the needs of each type.

The brokenhearted will be bandaged or bound up. Jesus promises to bind our broken hearts, stemming the pain and protecting us from further brokenness. Do you have a broken heart? Write out a short prayer asking the Mighty God to bind you up.

The captives will be set free by Jesus. We can become enslaved by many things, including our own toxic thinking. We tell ourselves lies such as, "I'm not capable enough," "I'm not smart enough," or "I'm not good enough." God knows we are "enough." God doesn't create junk people. All of us have purpose. What toxic thinking have you embraced about yourself? Do you believe you are not "enough?" Write out a short prayer asking Jesus, the Strength of God, to help you replace that toxic thinking with His true word about you.

The prisoners will be released from darkness. Prisoners are those who have sinned against society, and no matter how much they've hurt others, they truly are those in greatest darkness. Is there a darkness enveloping you? Do you long to be in the light? Write a prayer asking Jesus to shed His light on you and release you from this dark place.

What God is saying to me....

8

REVELATION 1:14-17

The hair on his head was white like wool, as white as snow, and his eyes were like blazing fire. His feet were like bronze glowing in a furnace, and his voice was like the sound of rushing waters. In his right hand he held seven stars, and coming out of his mouth was a sharp, double-edged sword. His face was like the sun shining in all its brilliance. When I saw him, I fell at his feet as though dead. Then he placed his right hand on me and said: "Do not be afraid. I am the First and the Last."

The personality of Jesus is illustrated in this incredible picture. On the one hand, Jesus is frightful and powerful. He peers at us with glowing eyes that can sear our souls, speaking words like a sharp sword cutting into our secret, hidden hearts with a blazing, eye-scorching face, footsteps melting obstacles as He strides His earth. He is the Truth of God.

On the other hand, listen to the peaceful sound of His voice, like a gentle River of Life. See him bending over and reaching out to lift us up with His Holy hands, whispering: don't be afraid. Encouraging us to remember Him, to know and love Him, and cling for our very lives to the omnipresent Everlasting Father, the Loyal One who will never leave us: The Grace of God.

Jesus is full of grace and full of truth at the same time. He is perfectly balanced, fully integrated in a way that we can only begin to understand. That such a God could love us with all His Majestic Heart, all His Noble Soul, all His Splendid Mind, and all His Renowned Strength is too much for us to even comprehend. And yet, simply, He does.

Which aspect of Jesus' personality do you need today? Is it His Truth – revealed in the Mighty God and the Wonderful Counselor? Or is it His Grace – found in the Everlasting Father and the Prince of Peace? Where do you need a touch by the Masterful King of Kings?

For more details on the complete, balanced personality of Jesus, see my book, Making Peace with Prickly People. His four-fold personality is revealed throughout Scripture, beginning in Genesis and ending in Revelation. Visit www.pricklypeople.com more details.

What God is saying to me...

9
PHILIPPIANS 2:6-7

Who, being in the very nature God, did not consider equality with God something to be used to his own advantage; rather he made himself nothing by taking the very nature of a servant, being made in human likeness.

We usually look for advantages for ourselves in everything we do. Which university is the best choice for my degree? Which job offer will give me the best edge for advancement? How many activities should I enroll my kids in, so they can have a leg-up when they get to high school?

We grasp for our puny preferences while Jesus didn't consider His advantages. He was willing to walk away from all the assets of heaven: the throne, the angel servants, the power; and traded those majestic benefits for nothing. He took on the form of a lowly servant. He was made in human likeness.

We are made in the image of God, and Jesus was made in the image of people. The basic model of our personalities and Jesus' personality are the same. However, there are some glaring differences.

Jesus is the perfect well-rounded personality. Our individual personalities are far from perfect. He is the leaded crystal, we are the plastic imitation.

He is truly and honestly humble. He was willing to be unconsidered, left behind, unrecognized for who He is, given short shrift, unappreciated. All for us. That's humility.

Humility is undervalued in our culture. Humble people are not respected. Consider your advantages. What if you were asked to give up your recognition or value for the sake of another person? Would you give up your rewards and give them to someone who didn't work to deserve them? That's what Jesus did for us. How does knowing this make a difference for you?

What God is saying to me...

10

GALATIANS 5:19-21

It is obvious what kind of life develops out of trying to get your own way all the time: repetitive, love-less, cheap sex; a stinking accumulation of mental and emotional garbage; frenzied and joyless grabs for happiness; trinket gods; magic-show religion; paranoid loneliness; cutthroat competition; all-consuming-yet-never-satisfied wants; a brutal temper; an impotence to love or be loved; divided homes and divided lives; small-minded and lopsided pursuits; the vicious habit of depersonalizing everyone into a rival; uncontrolled and uncontrollable addictions; ugly parodies of community. I could go on. (MSG)

Let's face it, our inborn selfishness gives birth to a dizzying variety of sins. Our selfish sin nature appears very early in life, when as toddlers we scream, "mine!" Think of the hours we take to patiently teach our babies to say "mama." We repeat this over and over with our faces close to the little cherubs. "Say mama!" We hopefully intone the syllables and are thrilled beyond belief the first time we hear that treasured title repeated. But who in their right mind ever practiced this language lesson with the word "mine?" And yet those little stinkers grasp this word with no problem at all.

Our sin causes a wall of separation between God and us. We want what we can't have - power, recognition, status, etc. It's just part of our nature. As we mature our needs hopefully diminish. But until Heaven, they'll still hang on.

The wall of separation between us and God can only be broken down by extreme measures. Death was required to end sin, because death is required to put an end to the insanity.

What area of sin is most tempting to you? Prayerfully read over the Scripture passage and ask God where you get tripped most often. What do other people see in you? Do they recognize you as the angry one, or the one who needs love, or the one who picks sides? If you're brave enough, show this passage to someone close to you and ask them which description most defines their perception of you.

What God is saying to me....

11

MATTHEW 27:46

My God, My God, why have You forsaken Me?

After three years of ministry and preparation, Jesus was ready to enter the battle of eternity. He went to the cross to die for our sinful selfishness. He suffered in every way possible: physically, emotionally, spiritually, and mentally.

There was only one agony that He mentioned on the cross, found in the Scripture passage above.

After proclaiming that He and the Father were One during His life, suddenly they are no longer One during His death.

On the cross, Jesus became sin, and God cannot be in relationship with sin. God doesn't play favorites, not even with His son.

Think about this – what if God had decided, just for this one time, that He could be in relationship with sin? After all, Jesus did everything He was supposed to do. He didn't deserve to die. Even though it cost both of them everything, the Father resolutely turned His back on Jesus at the hour of His greatest need.

I wonder what the angels in heaven thought as they observed this astounding scene. They must have held their breath, wondering if the broken Oneness would cause the entire universe to burst apart at the seams. This terrible price was paid so God would never have to turn His back on His beloved people, once they embraced His gift.

Have you ever experienced abandonment? That emotional pain is one of the most devastating we can feel. We were created for relationship and can face almost anything if we know we're not alone.

Jesus knows exactly what it feels like to be abandoned. That's why He promises in Hebrews 13:5, "I will never leave you."

What does it mean to you to know He will never abandon you?

What God is saying to me...

PART TWO:
LOVE SELF

12

ROMANS 12:6-7

We have different gifts, according to the grace given to each of us. If your gift is prophesying, then prophesy in accordance with your faith; if it is serving, then serve; if it is teaching, then teach.

Oswald Chambers mentioned personality in many of his writings. "Personality is that peculiar, incalculable thing that is meant when we speak of ourselves as distinct from everyone else." The Bible compares our different personality gifts to the individual parts of the human body. Each is unique and useful for its purpose.

The greatest commandment is to love God with all our heart (emotionally), all our soul (spiritually), all our mind (intellectually), and all our strength (productively). We are to love God with our entire four-fold personality.

Personality theory started with the ancient writings of Hippocrates, a Greek doctor born in 460 BC. He believed man had a four-fold personality, naming the styles sanguine, phlegmatic, melancholy, and choleric.

What are your gifts? Have you discovered that sweet spot in your being – something you excel at and gives you intense pleasure while serving others? Consider the path you've taken in life – even if you don't know your individual personality, chances are you've chosen a path that reflects what you really like to do. Your path gives clues about your personality.

If you haven't done so yet, visit www.pricklypeople.com and take the free Personality Key assessment. How is your personality reflected in your lifestyle, career, or relationships? After taking the test, you can sign up to receive a free report giving you more information about your gifts.

What God is saying to me....

13

DEUTERONOMY 6:6-9

These commandments that I give you today are to be on your hearts. Impress them on your children. Talk about them when you sit at home and when you walk along the road, when you lie down and when you get up. Tie them as symbols on your hands and bind them on your foreheads. Write them on the doorframes of your houses and on your gates.

The "commandments" above are called the "Shem'a." Jesus repeated the Shem'a in Mark 12. It goes like this: "Hear, O Israel: the Lord our God, the Lord is one. Love the Lord your God with all your heart and with all your soul and with all your strength" (Deuteronomy 6:4-5).

It's human nature to forget something if we don't see it or talk about it often enough, "out of sight out of mind."

We all need reminders of God's truth. Knowing and remembering who He is and who we are is critical for our faithfulness in carrying out our life mission. We are each created with gifts that God intends us to use for His glory. If we don't know His identity or our own, we will never be able to fulfill our mission on earth.

Deuteronomy 6 gives us some tips on how to keep God's commandments front and center in our minds. These constant reminders will help us go from knowing stuff about God in our heads to knowing stuff about God in our hearts. Which one of these will you start to practice today?

Teach them to other people.

Talk about them at home.

Talk about them when you're not at home.

Pray them as you go to sleep.

Pray them as you wake up.

Wear symbols of God's word.

Post them where you will see them daily.

What God is saying to me...

14

GENESIS 1:27

So God created mankind in his own image, in the image of God he created them; male and female he created them.

None of us has a perfect personality like Jesus, but we are all created in the image of God. As we explore who we are, we begin to see threads of Jesus' personality: The Heart, Soul, Mind, and Strength of God.

Our heart, soul, mind, and strength are not exactly like Jesus's. We are tainted by our sin nature. So our personality styles become "sanguine heart," "phlegmatic soul", "melancholy mind", and "choleric strength."

The sanguine heart is our emotional part. When this part is preferred, we are open, friendly, and motivating. We are optimistic and see the good in every person. We live in the moment.

The phlegmatic soul is our deep philosophical part. When we prefer to be soulish, we are easy going, humble, and adaptable. Our chief desire is to be free of conflict. We live inside our heads.

The melancholy mind is the intellectual part. Preferring this style means we are detail-oriented, careful, and perfectionistic. Conscientious is a good way to describe us. We live in the past.

The choleric strength part is the productive self. We could be known as "strong-willed." These are the leaders, the problem-solvers. We live in the future.

Ask several people you know which description best describes you. Are you surprised at their evaluation? Does it match your assessment results?

What God is saying to me...

15

JOHN 21:15

When they had finished eating, Jesus said to Simon Peter, "Simon son of John, do you love me more than these?" "Yes, Lord," he said, "you know that I love you." Jesus said, "Feed my lambs."

Peter is a great Biblical example of a sanguine heart personality. He, above all the other apostles, was the emotional one. He was first to blurt out his undying but naïve love for Christ. He was the only one to jump out of the boat and attempt to walk on water. He was among the inner circle of Jesus' closest confidantes, and yet was the only one to curse Jesus' name to his face.

The sanguine heart can be very naïve and impulsive. If this is your preferred personality style, do you sometimes wonder if you'll ever get your foot out of your mouth? Are you forgetful, always living in the moment?

People love the sanguine heart personality. They are fun to be around, but maybe not treated with respect by more intellectual people. Their child-like wonder can become childish behavior.

As a Christian, we always want to be progressing to become more like Christ. Studying Peter shows us how he learned from his mistakes and became a leader in the early church.

What do you consider your greatest sanguine flaws? Are you impetuous like Peter? Do you love to talk so much you forget God gave you only one mouth, but two ears? Are you quick to volunteer for projects and then struggle to follow through? Do you love getting to know people so much you forget to touch base with old friends, leaving them to wonder why you don't care anymore?

Peter eventually grew out of his impetuous nature, he became more realistic about his abilities. That's all Jesus is looking for, the mark of leadership is humility. Pray about your greatest flaw and ask God to temper you so you can become the leader he designed you to be.

What God is saying to me...

PHLEGMATIC SOUL

16

GENESIS 16:1-5

Now Sarai, Abram's wife, had borne him no children. But she had an Egyptian slave named Hagar; so she said to Abram, "The Lord has kept me from having children. Go, sleep with my slave; perhaps I can build a family through her." Abram agreed...He slept with Hagar, and she conceived. When she knew she was pregnant, she began to despise her mistress. Then Sarai said to Abram, "You are responsible for the wrong I am suffering..."

Abram never expected to be in such a pickle. He is a great example of a phlegmatic soul personality in the Bible. From the beginning of his story, we see his desire to avoid conflict and be a peace maker. But conflict avoidance can result in compromising our beliefs, which gets us into trouble.

Even though Abram had many flaws, God still chose him and trained him to become a leader and the "father of many nations." One of the gifts of the phlegmatic is loyalty, and Abram was loyal to God even though he stumbled with compromise several times in his life. Eventually Abram was able to stand up for his beliefs, always balanced with a gentle touch of mediation.

Is conflict-avoidance and compromise a snare for you? God isn't asking us to be perfect, but to model ourselves after the Perfect One. You are created in His image, and if this is your preferred style, He loves your phlegmatic 'soulishness.'

It's not time to throw in the towel when we fail to react to our struggles like Christ would, but it's a yellow caution flag. Ask God daily to give you awareness of unhealthy compromise. When you find yourself giving in, stop, and change direction. Ask God for forgiveness, pick yourself up, and move on. Rehearse the situation and how you could have responded so the next time you will stand strong in the face of opposition. In what situations are you most likely to compromise? Is there a prickly person in your life that makes you want to run and hide?

I was told in high school I should join the debate club. I wondered why anyone would join a club just to argue? I realize now how helpful it would have been to learn how to stand up for my principles. Look for opportunities where you could practice defending your beliefs.

What God is saying to me...

17
EXODUS 4:11-14

The Lord said to Moses, "Who gave human beings their mouths? Who makes them deaf or mute? Who gives them sight or makes them blind? Is it not I, the Lord? Now go; I will help you speak and will teach you what to say." But Moses said, "Pardon your servant, Lord. Please send someone else." Then the Lord's anger burned against Moses.

Moses had a brilliant mind, an excellent education, and many advantages that his fellow Hebrews lacked. He had leadership written all over him. Yet when God asks Moses to lead His people out of Egypt, Moses has one excuse after the other. Moses' problem? Fear.

Moses prefers the melancholy mind personality style. He is an intellectual and illustrates his abilities by writing the first five books of the Bible, being responsible for upholding the Ten Commandments, and acting as the General Contractor for the huge Tabernacle project. He's a perfectionist, detail-oriented, and sensitive as many melancholy types are.

For all his gifts, Moses has a major flaw – his fear. He is filled with self-doubt which almost derails him and his people, and results in what must have been the greatest disappointment of his life – getting left behind when his people finally reached the Promised Land.

Do you struggle with fear or self-doubt? They say that our greatest fear is the fear of the unknown. However, there really is no "unknown." God is omniscient, meaning He is all knowing. There is nothing He doesn't know. What we really fear is the fear of the unknown-to-me.

If you prefer the melancholy mind style, you are more intellectual, more detail oriented, more careful than most. God created you that way for a reason! He has important work for you to do and your gifts are exactly what is needed for that job. The only thing that can hold you back is your fear – what you don't know.

Is God calling you to something you fear? What is it? Write down all you don't know about your calling. Then write down all you do know. Pray and ask God to give you the faith to trust Him with your unknowns.

What God is saying to me....

18

ACTS 9:1,20-21

Meanwhile, Saul was still breathing out murderous threats against the Lord's disciples...

...At once he began to preach in the synagogues that Jesus is the Son of God. All those who heard him were astonished and asked, "Isn't he the man who raised havoc in Jerusalem among those who call on this name?"

Saul, or Paul as he was known after his conversion, illustrates the zeal and leadership skills of those who prefer the choleric strength style. He did everything 100%.

Paul was quick to make decisions. He immediately transformed from a Jesus-hater to a Jesus-lover after being struck blind. He was tireless in his campaign to spread the Gospel, he founded more churches than any other apostle, and authored most of the New Testament. If you had met him, you might think, "Is he for real?"

If you prefer the choleric strength style, people may say that about you. This style is the achiever, the "energizer bunny," the one who has bountiful energy and charisma. They make quick decisions, and love to achieve goals.

Sometimes we think a mature Christ follower must be more "soft," someone who might sit around the campfire singing "Kum-bay-a" and memorizing Scripture all day long. The choleric strength style doesn't like to sit and soak as much as other styles, they prefer to be on the move. But that's ok.

If this is your style, the world needs you! We need leaders who are motivating and inspiring and will take bold action. There is so much work to be done for the Kingdom!

At the same time, we all need to be filled by Jesus and equipped by His word to grow as Christians. Find ways to be filled that fit with your lifestyle. Memorize Scripture while walking on a treadmill, listen to your favorite Psalms on your audio Bible while running. Lead a small group of people you work with. What one step will you take this month to make sure you get fed by God while living your active lifestyle?

What God is saying to me....

19
EPHESIANS 4:15

Instead, speaking the truth in love, we will grow to become in every respect the mature body of him who is the head, that is, Christ.

This Scripture gives an example of Christian maturity – speaking truth in love. Most of us either prefer to speak truth or speak love. Christ was the only one who could consistently do both. He's our role model.

The choleric and melancholy styles might excel at speaking truth. Truth is important, we want to evaluate the problem, then we want to fix the problem without emotions getting in the way. We want to make sure the rules are followed, and don't appreciate drama. It just prevents us from getting our work done!

On the other hand, the sanguine and phlegmatic styles prefer to speak love. They see the relationship as the most critical element in solving problems. They want to preserve the team-spirit, avoid conflict, and find consensus.

No matter what our preferred personality style, we can all grow in this most basic rule of communication: speak truth in love. Which side of the equation is most challenging to you?

If you love to speak truth, here is a suggestion. Before "telling it like it is," try sandwiching your suggestion for improvement with praises. "I really appreciate that you got the work done on time. Could you go over this report and make sure you edit for grammar mistakes? I know the staff is going to be pleased to read your results."

If you usually speak love, try the same method. You will probably have no trouble praising someone. Sandwich your praises with your truthful assessment of the situation. You'll find most people appreciate your honest opinion when it's couched in love.

What current situation or relationship could improve if you spoke truth in love? Try writing out what you will say using the techniques above.

What God is saying to me....

20

1 CORINTHIANS 13:11A

When I was a child, I talked like a child, I thought like a child, I reasoned like a child.

Children talk, think, and reason like children. And when we encounter confusing or difficult situations in childhood we are likely to come to childish conclusions. We have limited knowledge and the adults in our lives may be too busy or too broken to help us understand. Many of our childish conclusions are about our own identity and may be wrong. Those lies can become the bedrock of who we believe we are.

Thinking back to your childhood, what were your defining moments? Can you recall situations or relationships that made you think you were not smart enough, not good enough, not pretty enough, or just not enough? Some of our defining moments came from the careless words of an angry or busy or frustrated adult. For some of us, defining moments were heartbreaking abuse or loss. My false identity as a child included these axioms:

My words hurt people.

I don't know what I'm talking about.
I better just be quiet.

Without realizing it, I "put on a mask" and took on a false identity, exactly opposite of the way God designed me.

The passage quoted above ends like this: "When I became a man, I put the ways of childhood behind me" (1 Corinthians 13:11b). Now that we are adults, we can choose what to believe. We can choose to evaluate our identity, accept the parts that line up with God's word, and reject those that don't.

No matter how angry or busy or frustrated your parents were, you can now parent yourself. What erroneous conclusions did you arrive at as a child? Pray and ask God to reveal your true identity, as He defines you. Reject the false axioms as you become aware of them. When you understand your true identity, you may be as astonished as I was. God has shown me who I really am.

I am empathetic, my words don't hurt people, they help people.
I have a good mind, I do know what I'm talking about.
I was made to tell the story, I better not just be quiet!

What God is saying to me...

21
EPHESIANS 2:10

For we are God's handiwork, created in Christ Jesus to do good works, which God prepared in advance for us to do.

We are God's handiwork; the word "handiwork" in Greek is "poiema." This is where our word poetry comes from. What a magnificent picture of how God defines those who follow Him. God calls His followers an epic masterpiece, a moving sonnet, an exquisite opus.

God begins to transform us as we yield to Him, being brave about accepting our failures, confessing regularly to ask forgiveness, and believing that we are forgiven. We partner with God in a way. He gives us free will and we can choose to grow more like Him or to stay stuck in our false identity.

The following list of Scriptures reveals our identity in Christ. Note that each sentence is written in the present tense; it's not that we will become like this, it is our identity now.

As you read over the Scriptures, which ones do you struggle to believe are true for you today?

- You are filled with the peace and joy of God (John 14:27, Romans 14:17).

- You are God's beloved child (John 1:12, Ephesians 1:5).

- You are completely forgiven, perfectly righteous, and free from condemnation (Romans 5:1, 1 Corinthians 6:20, Ephesians 1:7).

- You are God's glorious temple and are filled with his fullness (1 Corinthians 6:19, Ephesians 3:19).

- You are the beautiful bride of Christ who ravishes the heart of God (Song of Songs 4:1-15, Ephesians 5:25-32).

- You are indwelled by a fearless Spirit of love and self-control (2 Timothy 1:7).

- You are more than a conqueror in all things (Romans 8:37).

How would it change your life if you really believed these words? Write out a prayer asking God to help you believe these truths and reject the lies that are blocking your true identity.

What God is saying to me...

PART THREE: LOVE THEM

22

EPHESIANS 4:26-27

In your anger do not sin: do not let the sun go down while you are still angry, and do not give the devil a foothold.

Why are prickly relationships so difficult? It seems that we keep trying over and over to improve a relationship, but nothing ever changes. Over time, as we hold onto anger and bitterness, our enemy gets a foothold in us. Our anger develops into stinky, rotten contempt.

Feeling contempt for someone is the utmost pride and arrogance. Contempt is feeling we're better than someone else. But contempt is one of our enemy's greatest lies. In God's economy, no one is better than anyone else. We are all on a level playing field. We are all sinners, even if we have been saved by grace. If I've allowed contempt to grow in me, I not only have a problem with Prickly, I also have a problem with God.

Most of us struggle to heal relationships because we only focus on getting along with that person. But if contempt has snuck into our hearts, we need to go vertical and confess our contempt to God. We need to make peace with God before we can make peace with Prickly.

Think about a relationship you would like to improve. Ask yourself these questions, prayerfully and honestly.

In what ways do you show respect to this person?

Do you gossip about or slander this person in front of others?

When others praise this person do you remain silent and wonder who they're talking about?

When this person makes a mistake would you be likely to think, "that's just like him."

Contempt is like drinking poison and expecting the other person to die, it's physically unhealthy. Consider reading Making Peace with Prickly People and going through the study guide to find healing and peace in your life.

What God is saying to me....

23

MATTHEW 6:14-15

For if you forgive other people when they sin against you, your heavenly Father will also forgive you. But if you do not forgive others their sins, your Father will not forgive your sins.

Forgiveness is a complex concept to understand. God's definition of forgiveness is very different from the world's definition, so confusion abounds.

The forgiveness written about here is not optional. God requires us to forgive people in a vertical sense. Vertical forgiveness is an agreement between me and God that I will not treat the other person they way they deserve to be treated.

God requires this form of forgiveness from us when we have been forgiven by Him. When we become Christ followers, our sins are forgiven by the blood of Jesus. That forgiveness is a powerful and rich gift. It carries a certain responsibility with it, though. God challenges us to forgive others that same way.

When God forgives us, He doesn't say it didn't matter, or that we really didn't sin. He merely agrees not to treat us the way we deserve to be treated and accepts us into His family.

When we forgive others, we are not accepting the blame for their sin, we aren't saying it was ok, not a big deal. Our vertical forgiveness is an agreement between us and God that we will not treat the other person the way they deserve to be treated.

Many people think they cannot forgive someone because they can never forget. Forgiveness isn't the same thing as amnesia. God doesn't develop amnesia, but what He 'forgets' is His need to punish us for them, He 'forgets' His anger toward us.

When I've forgiven someone, I don't lose my memory. But gradually, I can think about that situation without getting angry. That's how I know I have finally forgiven. I've forgotten my anger at them.

Are you angry with someone? Begin to vertically forgive them by promising God you will stop talking and thinking about it. Ask Him for help in keeping this promise. It's not easy but it can be done.

What God is saying to me...

24

ROMANS 12:18

If it is possible, as far as it depends on you, live at peace with everyone.

In contrast to vertical forgiveness, this passage refers to another type: horizontal forgiveness. Horizontal forgiveness is between two people. One person was hurt by the antagonist. The antagonist must ask for forgiveness and the injured person must grant forgiveness. It requires two people to cooperate.

The person who wronged us may never admit fault and may not ask for forgiveness. One of the most frustrating lessons I've learned is that we can't change other people. We can't force them to be remorseful about hurting us. And God knows this, we are not responsible for the actions of another person.

God graciously gives us an out with this type of forgiveness. Note there are conditions given, that it may not be possible, and it doesn't just depend on us. God wants all His people to live in peace, but if it isn't possible, He doesn't require horizontal forgiveness.

If you have a difficult relationship, have you tried everything possible? Are you willing to change your approach, to soften your words or attitudes? Can you give a little? Remember that while we may not have started the conflict, we are responsible for our response. We can still own our part in a prickly situation because of our disrespectful, dishonoring or unloving response.

The Bible instructs us to honor our parents, respect our spouses, and love our enemies. The Bible doesn't give any qualifying conditions. We are to honor our parents whether they act in honorable ways or not. We are to respect our husbands whether they act respectably or not. We are to love our enemies even when they are quite unlovable.

Even if you have done everything possible to be at peace with someone, things may not change. The relationship may be irreconcilable. You will not receive peace from that person, but you can receive peace anyway, peace from God that doesn't make sense from an earthly standpoint. He is ready to meet every need you have, through Jesus Christ. What need have you been wanting your prickly person to meet? Can you give that to God instead? What one thing can you do today to attempt to live at peace with your prickly person?

What God is saying to me...

25

MATTHEW 10:39B

Whoever loses their life for my sake will find it.

Boundaries are meant to keep the good in and the bad out. Healthy relationships require healthy boundaries.

Vertical forgiveness is required in our relationships, as we promise not to bring up the subject with them, others, or ourselves. But trust is not required, and it is healthy to put a boundary between you and another person if, or until, they can be trusted again.

Physical boundaries have to do with how others may touch us and under what conditions. Mental boundaries give us the freedom to have our own thoughts and opinions. Emotional boundaries allow us to disengage from the manipulative emotions of others. And spiritual boundaries help us distinguish God's will for ourselves, which are not based on anyone else's will for us.

Sometimes having low boundaries is confused with being selfless. We are encouraged to live selflessly in Scripture, so what's the difference between selflessness and low boundaries?

Jesus gives us the answer in the passage above. The key is the phrase, 'for my sake.' When choosing to give up our rights or needs for the sake of Jesus, then we find New Life: the abundant, over-flowing life of Christ. That's living sacrificially and selflessly for Him. In what ways have you given up something in your life for His sake?

Having low boundaries is like losing our life (or rights or needs) for another person. It's failing to care for ourselves for the sake of someone else (This goes way beyond giving up sleep to care for a sick child, it is feeling that your worth as a person is less than someone else's worth). If we give up ourselves, our needs, or our rights for the sake of another person, we are in an unhealthy position. We all have people we are entrusted to care for: children, aging parents, spouses. But have you ever gone beyond that norm? Have you felt that your purpose on earth was to fulfill another person? Ask God to help you to set appropriate boundaries with them, and to live for Him only.

What God is saying to me...

26
JAMES 1:2-4

Consider it pure joy, my brothers and sisters, whenever you face [prickly people] of many kinds, because you know that the testing of your faith produces perseverance. Let perseverance finish its work so that you may be mature and complete, not lacking anything (my translation).

Pure joy is rarely experienced by me in a prickly relationship, to be honest. But that's because my perspective isn't God's perspective.

Many things test my faith, but difficult relationships are the most challenging test of all. Everything we do is done in relationship, whether in family settings, education, career, service, or retirement. Unless you live as a hermit, you are going to have to exist in relationship to someone.

In what ways has your faith been tested by relationships? We all want to be mature and complete as this passage promises. Perseverance is the quality that contributes to our completeness. A person who perseveres is not distracted from his purpose and faith by even the greatest of sufferings.

Sometimes our relationships do produce suffering: undeserved and unfair slights and hurts. But sometimes, our suffering can be magnified by our own smarting pride.

Is there any chance your prickly person is like a mirror, showing you an area where you aren't mature or complete? None of us want to take a long look in the mirror, right? We don't want to see our flaws. But everyone else does!

I don't know about you, but when someone corrects me, my first instinct is to justify myself or correct them back. But if I stop, consider, and ask God what He wants me to learn from this correction, maybe I will gain something, becoming more mature and complete.

Emerson Eggerichs says that when we are hurt by someone else, it's like they stepped on us. If we are a rose-like person, a beautiful aroma will arise when we are 'stepped on.' But if we are a skunk-like person, a stench will arise when we are 'stepped on.' Which are you, a skunk or a rose?

What God is saying to me....

27

EPHESIANS 6:12

For our struggle is not against flesh and blood, but against the rulers, against the authorities, against the powers of this dark world and against the spiritual forces of evil in the heavenly realms.

Making peace with prickly people can be like living in a war zone. If you're like me, you've been battling in one conflict after the other all your life. Sometimes the skirmishes are few and far between, and sometimes one spills over into another and our lives become continual chaos. But it's critical to know your true enemy in this chaos.

This passage of Scripture reveals who the true enemy is. My prickly person is not my true foe, neither is my husband, my in-law; it's not my child, my sibling, or my employer.

Sometimes we seem to take a stand against another person, with our sword drawn and shield at the ready. When we get poked, we jab back. Every comment, every shrug, every raised eyebrow puts us on the defensive. We walk around, battle-ready, twenty-four-seven. The stress of living this way paralyzes us. We shield our hearts so efficiently that eventually they become hard and cold and unfeeling to everyone and everything.

In what ways does this describe you? You might be experiencing physical symptoms of stress such as insomnia, digestive problems, allergies, back pain, etc. Some researchers believe up to 95% of all physical disease begins with stress.

Our true enemy is Satan. He gloats and giggles when we harbor hate and contempt toward other people. He is thrilled when we engage with the wrong foe, leaving our families broken and our bodies weakened. Satan can sit back and sneer with delight.

Have you been battling the wrong enemy? How does it change your perspective to know who your true enemy is? What one thing can you choose to do today to let down your guard against your prickly person? (Note: if you are being abused or are in danger with this person, don't attempt to let down your guard! Instead get somewhere safe and get help.)

What God is saying to me....

28

JOHN 16:11

The prince of this world now stands condemned.

The prince of this world is our enemy Satan. And he is already condemned by God. Hell was created for him and his cohorts. They each have a cell with their name on the door, just waiting for God to lock them up. Satan truly has no power nor any authority, for all power and authority was given to Christ.

Satan is not very creative, he really has only one trick up his sleeve: lies. If he can get us to believe lies about God, about ourselves, or about other people, he has succeeded.

Here are some characteristics of our enemy, our true prickly person:

- He lies, and he's the father of lies (John 8:44)

- He is disobedient (Ephesians 2:2)

- He is full of darkness and wickedness (Ephesians 6:12)

- He doubts our goodness (Job 1:9)

- He is crafty and smart (Genesis 3:1)

- He loves to deceive us by hinting that God's truth is too simple to be true. (2 Corinthians 11:3)

- He is a master of disguise, and will even pose as an angel of light (2 Corinthians 11:4)

- He has free reign on the earth (Job 2:2)

Even though our true prickly person seems so impossible to overpower, we know he is already condemned: "the prince of this world stands condemned." The battle for eternity is a done deal – signed, sealed, and completed at the resurrection of Jesus. We know he can trick us, deceive us, lie to us, but he cannot make us sin. Our response is our responsibility. We know if we resist him, he will flee (James 4:7). We don't have to fear this prickly person because God has already taken care of him.

Which of God's truths do you doubt? What lies have you believed about God, about yourself, or about other people? Will you confess your failure to believe God's truth today? Will you replace that lie you believed with the truth?

What God is saying to me....

29
REVELATION 19:9

Blessed are those who are invited to the wedding supper of the Lamb!

Weddings are big business in the United States, capturing $50 billion yearly of our hard-earned money. Cha-Ching! There's something about the feasting, the music, the special-ness of getting dressed up and celebrating that appeals to us. Weddings appeal to God too. But for God, it's about so much more than the dress and the flowers. God is planning the wedding to end all weddings – the Marriage Supper of the Lamb.

In heaven, a huge celebration will mark the beginning of a new era. Chapter 19 of Revelation describes some of the events of this incredible day. A great multitude will raise their voices together, sounding like thunder and waterfalls, praising and glorifying Jesus, the Lamb of God. The wedding guests will be clothed in fine white linen, bright and clean. These clothes will symbolize our righteous and holy lives. It truly will be a blessing to be invited to this marvelous marriage supper. No one will want to miss it.

Picture yourself on that day, dressed in fine white linen, excitement making your heart pound a little harder, anticipation for the festivities sparkling in your eyes. As you prepare for this feast, grab your invitation and make your way to the Great Hall, will you have any regrets? Will you feel a tinge of sadness because someone is going to be missing from this wedding to end all weddings?

Will you wonder if their absence has anything to do with your anger toward them? Who do you know that is at risk of not being invited? Can you ask yourself today – why is this person in my life, Lord? Do you want to invite them to the Marriage Supper of the Lamb? How can I help them receive Your invitation?

Anticipate your attendance at this amazing event. And consider donating your pride, your forgiveness, and your peace-keeping efforts towards the invitation for your prickly person. You will never regret it.

What God is saying to me....

30

1 JOHN 4:7-8

Dear friends, let us love one another, for love comes from God. Everyone who loves has been born of God and knows God. Whoever does not love does not know God, because God is love.

Love comes from God. God is love. We cannot love unless we first receive the love of God and learn to love Him back in the same way. Love is the litmus test for those who know God. If someone loves sacrificially and unconditionally, we know they have been born of God. If someone does not love unconditionally they don't truly know God. These people may know about God, but they clearly don't know God.

When Jesus said in Mark 12 that the most important commandment is to love God with all our heart, all our soul, all our mind, and all our strength, He was letting us know that if we only get one thing right in this life, it's to love God.

We can't love God unless we truly know Him. If we learn all there is to know about George Washington, read every book written about him, study every letter and missive he left behind, we will be able to say we know about George Washington. But unless you were alive when he was alive, spoke to him, listened to him, you don't really know George Washington.

The same goes for God. We can study the Bible, memorize Scripture, attend and even write Bible studies, work full time in ministry, but unless we know God, we cannot love Him. Unless we love Him, we cannot love others.

No one can know George Washington now, since he has passed away. But God is knowable to anyone who wishes to know Him. "You will seek me and find me when you seek me with all your heart" (Jeremiah 29:13).

To make peace in any prickly relationship, we must always go to God first, to deepen and establish that love. Then we are equipped to love others as we love ourselves. How healthy is your love for God? How do you experience His love for you? If you are not sure start by praying to Him daily, asking Him to show you how to seek Him. Don't stop until you find him.

What God is saying to me....

ABOUT THE AUTHOR

DEB POTTS

If you enjoyed this short devotional, you will want to read Making Peace with Prickly People.

Visit www.pricklypeople.com for links to the print and eBook formats, as well as some free downloads including the Personality Key© assessment, a Prickly People Prayer Calendar, and a 6-week Bible study guide.

I am a Christian inspirational speaker, and I love to equip and encourage women to find exceptional life in Jesus. Contact me and let me know how I can serve your women's ministry group. Visit debpotts.com/contact.

ABOUT THE ARTIST

MACY SIMMONS

From a young age, I've always had a love for creating. What began as a way to ease boredom in school and make free birthday gifts for friends has led to an Etsy shop, and my first published art (Mindful)!

I currently live in Atlanta, Georgia, but was born and raised in Rochester, Michigan. I typically spend my days mentoring college students through my job with Athletes in Action, hanging with my awesome husband Solomon, and snuggling with my kitten.

If you are interested in more of my work, be sure to check out my website at https://www.etsy.com/shop/writtenontheheart423. I truly love knowing that through my shop, God's incredible truth can hang on the walls of homes throughout the country! I am always looking for new ways to create, so if you have any ideas or requests, feel free to email me at writtenontheheart423@gmail.com.

33075424R00041

Made in the USA
Columbia, SC
07 November 2018